ARIZONA CARDINALS

BY ALEX MONNIG

The Child's World®

Published by The Child's World®
1980 Lookout Drive • Mankato, MN 56003-1705
800-599-READ • www.childsworld.com

Acknowledgments
The Child's World®: Mary Berendes, Publishing Director
Red Line Editorial: Editorial direction
The Design Lab: Design

Design Element: Dean Bertoncelj/Shutterstock Images
Photographs ©: Mark Humphrey/AP Images, cover, 1;
Todd Kirkland/Icon Sportswire, 5; PCN/Corbis, 7;
Bettmann/Corbis, 9; Bruce Yeung/Icon Sportswire, 11,
25; Gene Lower/AP Images, 13; Rick Scuteri/AP Images,
14–15, 19; Paul Spinelli/AP Images, 17; Ross D. Franklin/
AP Images, 21; AP Images, 23; Zach Bolinger/Icon
Sportswire. 27; Art Phillips/Bettmann/Corbis, 29

ISBN 9781634070157
LCCN 2014959720

Printed in the United States of America
Mankato, MN
July, 2015
PA02265

ABOUT THE AUTHOR

Alex Monnig is a freelance journalist from St. Louis, Missouri, who now lives in Sydney, Australia. He has traveled across the world to cover sporting events in China, India, Singapore, New Zealand, and Scotland. No matter where he is, he always makes time to keep up to date with his favorite teams from his hometown.

TABLE OF CONTENTS

GO, CARDINALS!

The Arizona Cardinals have been around for more than 90 years. They are one of the oldest football teams. But they have had trouble winning. They have lost more games than any other team. The Cardinals have made the playoffs only nine times through 2014. But they still have plenty of fans who love them. Let's meet the Cardinals!

Cardinals running back Andre Ellington (38) rushes against the Atlanta Falcons on November 30, 2014.

WHO ARE THE CARDINALS?

The Cardinals play in the National Football League (NFL). They are one of the 32 teams in the NFL. The NFL includes the American Football Conference (AFC) and the National Football Conference (NFC). The winner of the NFC plays the winner of the AFC in the Super Bowl. The Cardinals play in the West Division of the NFC. The Cardinals have been to the Super Bowl only once, and they lost. They won two NFL championships before the Super Bowl was created.

Cardinals quarterback Kurt Warner (13) drops back to pass during the NFC wild-card playoff game against the Green Bay Packers on January 10, 2010.

WHERE THEY CAME FROM

The Cardinals played in Chicago from 1920 to 1959. They won the 1925 and 1947 NFL championships. Many players had to fight in World War II during the 1940s. In 1944, the Cardinals and the Pittsburgh Steelers combined rosters. They were called Card-Pitt.

The Cardinals moved to St. Louis in 1960. Fans there loved them. They played in the same **stadium** as Major League Baseball's Cardinals starting in 1960. Both teams moved to a new stadium in 1966. But owner Bill Bidwill wanted another new stadium in the late 1980s. So in 1987 he moved the team to Phoenix,

Halfback Charlie Trippi of the Chicago Cardinals rushes for six yards against the Washington Redskins on November 23, 1947.

Arizona. At first the team was called the Phoenix Cardinals. Then in 1994 they became the Arizona Cardinals.

WHO THEY PLAY

The Cardinals play 16 games each season. With so few games, each one is important. Every year, the Cardinals play two games against each of the other three teams in their division. They are the San Francisco 49ers, Seattle Seahawks, and St. Louis Rams. Arizona also plays six other teams from the NFC and four from the AFC.

Cardinals safety Tony Jefferson (22) celebrates with a teammate after sacking San Francisco 49ers quarterback Colin Kaepernick on September 21, 2014.

WHERE THEY PLAY

The Cardinals play in University of Phoenix Stadium. It is in Glendale, Arizona, a suburb of Phoenix. It has a roof that can open and close. In addition, the field can be moved outside between games. This allows the natural grass to grow in the sunlight. Up to 72,200 fans can fit in to watch games. The Cardinals started playing in the University of Phoenix Stadium in 2006. College football's Fiesta Bowl is played in the stadium each year. The stadium also hosted the Super Bowl after the 2007 and 2014 seasons.

There is enough concrete in University of Phoenix Stadium to pave a sidewalk that goes from Phoenix to San Francisco.

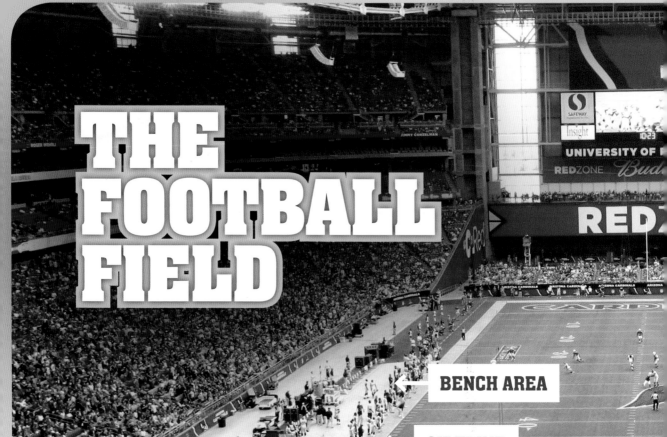

THE FOOTBALL FIELD

BENCH AREA

SIDELINE

GOAL POST

END ZONE

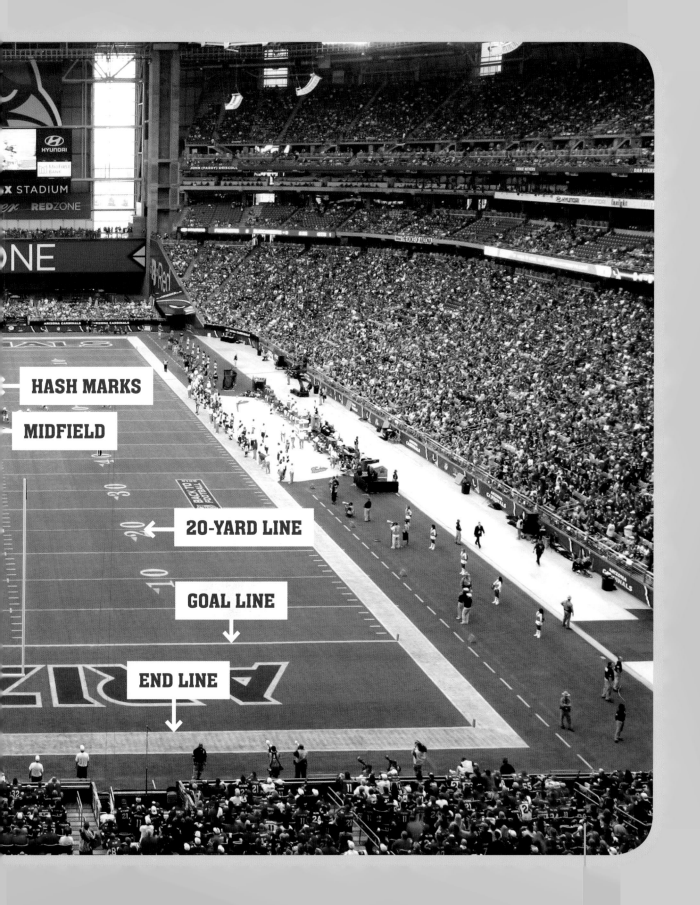

HASH MARKS

MIDFIELD

20-YARD LINE

GOAL LINE

END LINE

BIG DAYS

The Cardinals have had some great moments in their history. Here are three of the greatest:

1988—The Cardinals got their first home win in Arizona. They beat the Washington Redskins 30–21 on September 25.

2004—Emmitt Smith is one of the best running backs ever. He spent his last two seasons with Arizona. On October 24, Smith scored on a 23-yard run against the Seattle Seahawks. That gave him more than 100 rushing yards that day. That was the record-setting 78th time he had rushed for more than 100 yards in a game in his career.

Running back Tim Hightower (34) runs for the game-winning touchdown in the NFC Championship Game on January 18, 2009.

2009—On January 18, the 2008 Cardinals beat the Philadelphia Eagles 32–25 in the NFC Championship Game. Running back Tim Hightower scored on a touchdown pass from Kurt Warner with 2:59 left to win the game. That earned the Cardinals their first trip to the Super Bowl.

TOUGH DAYS

Football is a hard game. Even the best teams have rough games and rough seasons. Here are some of the toughest times in Cardinals history:

1944—The Card-Pitt team went 0-10. The team's home games were in Pittsburgh. Most Cardinals fans were not even able to go support their team. It was the Cardinals' second winless season in a row.

2010—Star quarterback Kurt Warner was injured in a playoff game against the New Orleans Saints on January 16. Warner never played again. Later people found out that Saints players were illegally being paid bonuses to try to hurt Warner.

Buffalo Bills defensive end Chris Kelsay sacks Cardinals quarterback Kevin Kolb on October 14, 2012.

2012—The Cardinals have lost a lot of games in their history. On October 14, the Buffalo Bills handed them another loss. That made the Cardinals the first team to lose 700 games.

MEET THE FANS

The Cardinals play in Arizona now. But they still have some fans in St. Louis. Some people there still miss the city's first football team. Cardinals fans have had to put up with a lot of losing. But they have stuck by their team. The Cardinals' mascot is a bird named Big Red. He has entertained the Arizona crowds since 1998.

Big Red joins Cardinals fans in a cheer during a preseason game against the San Diego Chargers on August 22, 2009.

HEROES THEN

Offensive lineman Dan Dierdorf played from 1971 to 1983. He was quick for a big man. He protected the quarterback and cleared the path for running backs. Dierdorf was a big reason why the Cardinals allowed just eight **sacks** in 14 games in 1975. That was an NFL record. Jackie Smith was an offensive star. He retired in 1978 with career records for most receptions (480), receiving yards (7,918), and **touchdowns** (40) by a tight end. Cornerback Aeneas Williams played for the Cardinals from 1991 to 2000. He made the **Pro Bowl** six times in that span. He led the league with nine interceptions in 1994.

Cardinals tight end Jackie Smith catches a pass against the Washington Redskins on October 24, 1965.

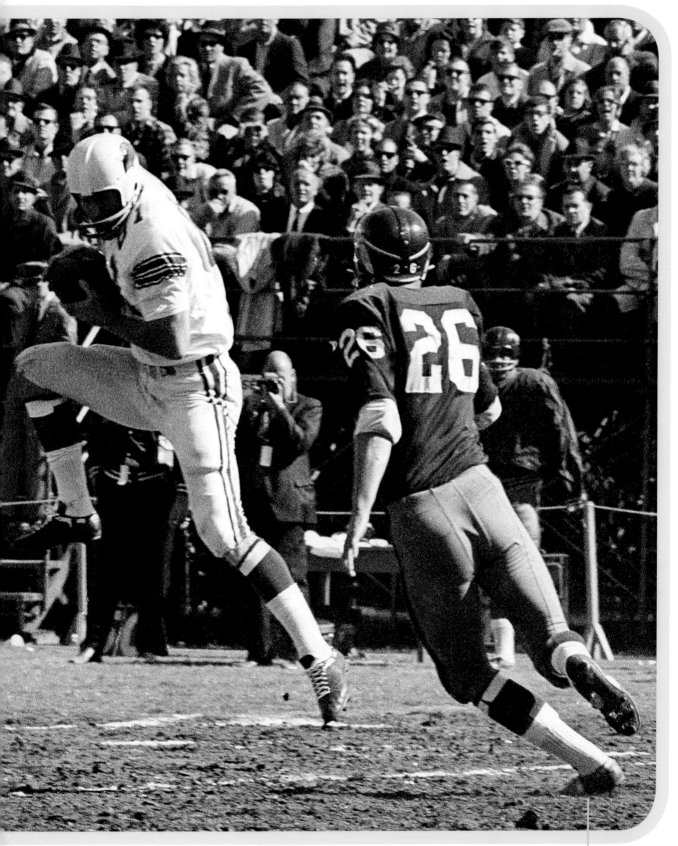

HEROES NOW

Larry Fitzgerald is the best wide receiver in team history. He is tall and famous for his acrobatic catches. He made eight Pro Bowls in his first ten seasons. Andre Ellington is an exciting running back. He is a fast runner who can also catch the ball. Ellington is small but dangerous in the open field. Cornerback Patrick Peterson helps the team on **defense** and **special teams**. He tied a record as a **rookie** in 2011 with four punt return touchdowns.

Cardinals wide receiver Larry Fitzgerald (11) runs with the ball during a 23–14 victory over the San Francisco 49ers on September 21, 2014.

GEARING UP

NFL players wear team uniforms. They wear helmets and pads to keep them safe. Cleats help them make quick moves and run fast. Some players wear extra gear for protection.

THE FOOTBALL

NFL footballs are made of leather. Under the leather is a lining that fills with air to give the ball its shape. The leather has bumps or "pebbles." These help players grip the ball. Laces help players control their throws. Footballs are also called "pigskins" because some of the first balls were made from pig bladders. Today they are made of leather from cows.

Running back Andre Ellington runs after catching a pass in a game against the Dallas Cowboys on November 2, 2014.

HELMET

SHOULDER PADS

GLOVES

THIGH PADS

FOOTBALL

CLEATS

SPORTS STATS

ere are some of the all-time career records for the Arizona Cardinals. All the stats are through the 2014 season.

RUSHING YARDS

Ottis Anderson 7,999

Stump Mitchell 4,649

TOTAL TOUCHDOWNS

Larry Fitzgerald 89

Roy Green 69

RECEPTIONS

Larry Fitzgerald 909

Anquan Boldin 586

INTERCEPTIONS

Larry Wilson 52

Aeneas Williams 46

SACKS

Freddie Joe Nunn 66.5

Simeon Rice 51.5

POINTS

Jim Bakken 1,380

Neil Rackers 699

Cardinals quarterback Jim Hart looks to pass during a game on October 28, 1979.

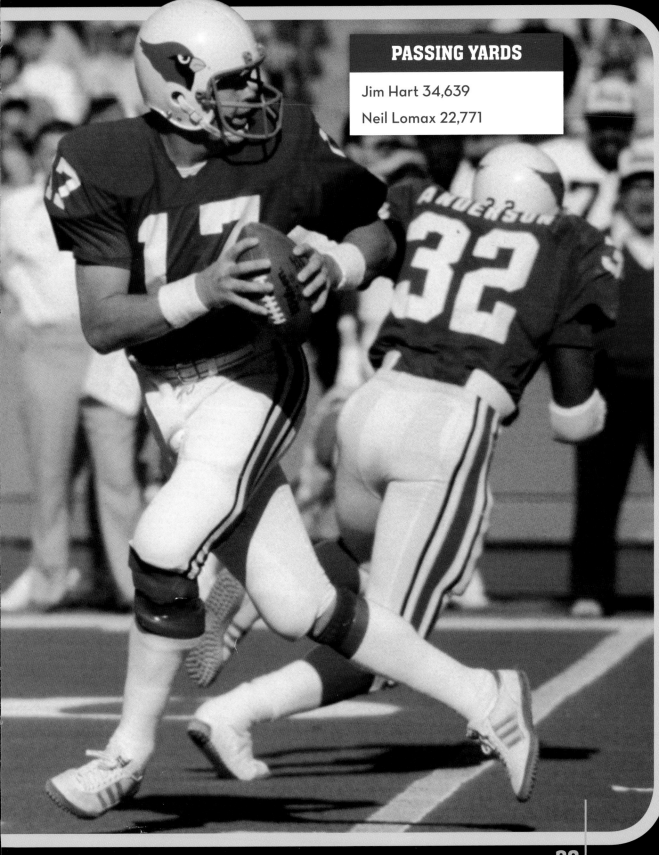

PASSING YARDS

Jim Hart 34,639

Neil Lomax 22,771

GLOSSARY

defense when a team doesn't have the ball and is trying to keep the other team from scoring

league an organization of sports teams that compete against each other

Pro Bowl the NFL's all-star game, in which the best players in the league compete

rookie a player playing in his first full season

sacks when the quarterback is tackled behind the line of scrimmage before he can throw the ball

special teams groups of players on the field during kicking plays

stadium a building with a field and seats for fans where teams play

touchdowns plays in which the ball is held in the other team's end zone, resulting in six points

FIND OUT MORE

IN THE LIBRARY

Gilbert, Sara. *The Story of the Arizona Cardinals.*
Mankato, MN: Creative Education, 2010.

Roberts, Russell. *Larry Fitzgerald.*
Hockessin, DE: Mitchell Lane, 2011.

Stewart, Mark. *The Arizona Cardinals.*
Chicago: Norwood House Press, 2013.

ON THE WEB

Visit our Web site for links about the Arizona Cardinals:
childsworld.com/links

Note to Parents, Teachers, and Librarians: We routinely verify our Web links to make sure they are safe and active sites. So encourage your readers to check them out!

INDEX